This or That

Questions About Storm Chasing

You Decide!

by Jaclyn Jaycox

Raintree is an imprint of Capstone Global Library Limited, a company incorporated in England and Wales having its registered office at 264 Banbury Road, Oxford, OX2 7DY – Registered company number: 6695582

www.raintree.co.uk
myorders@raintree.co.uk

Edited by Gena Chester
Designed by Heidi Thompson
Original illustrations © Capstone Global Library Limited 2022
Picture research by Jo Miller
Production by Tori Abraham
Originated by Capstone Global Library Ltd

978 1 3982 3453 6 (hardback)
978 1 3982 3455 0 (paperback)

British Library Cataloguing in Publication Data
A full catalogue record for this book is available from the British Library.

Acknowledgements
We would like to thank the following for permission to reproduce photographs: Getty Images: Jessica Moore, 17; Newscom: Reuters/GENE BLEVINS, 28, Reuters/STEVE MARCUS, 18, ZUMA Press/Mike Coniglio, 6; Science Source: Howard Bluestein, 21, Jim Reed, 16, 20, 26, 27; Shutterstock: aslysun, 29, ben bryant, 13, Cammie Czuchnicki, Cover (tornado), CDrnitry9131, Cover (camera), DedMityay, 11, Elena Helade, 10, FootMade0525, Cover (tree), GSW Photography, 4, Huntstyle, 8, John D Sirlin, 15, lafoto, 9, Lutic, 14, M Kunz, Cover (cow), Menno van der Haven, 3, Minerva Studio, 22, 23, Raquel Pedrosa, 19, Sandra Sapp, 25, Vladimir Nogales L, 12, William A. Morgan, 24, Wirestock Creators, 7. Design element: Shutterstock: Steven Wright, Cover (map).

Every effort has been made to contact copyright holders of material reproduced in this book. Any omissions will be rectified in subsequent printings if notice is given to the publisher.

Printed and bound in India.

Severe weather

Severe weather happens all around the world. Hurricanes can destroy coastal cities in places such as Australia, Japan, China and the United States. The United States is hit with more than 1,000 tornadoes each year. Severe thunderstorms can bring **hail** the size of golf balls and flash floods. Many people take cover during dangerous weather – but not storm chasers.

Most storm chasers are scientists who study the weather. They chase storms to learn more about them. The more scientists learn, the better they can **predict** the weather. Better predictions could help people be more prepared, which saves lives.

How to use this book

Storms can sweep through cities and knock down anything in their paths. Imagine you are a storm chaser. What sort of storms would you chase?

You are about to read questions related to surviving storm chasing. The questions are followed by information to help you make your decisions. Choose one or the other, but weigh your options carefully! Your life could depend on it.

✔ get close to dangerous storms

✔ spend hours or days driving

✔ study lots of data

Storm chasers seek out severe weather. Their goal is to get as close to the storm as safely as possible. This lets them gather **data**. They make up-close **observations**. They even place scientific equipment to get picked up by the storm. Chasers can spend hours, or even days, driving towards unstable weather. They constantly **monitor** weather reports. They study a lot of data to try to predict the path of the storm.

That? be a storm spotter

- ✔ little travel needed
- ✔ stay further away from storms
- ✔ can help make sure warnings are accurate

Storm spotters usually report on weather near their homes, so there is very little travel. They do not need to get close to storms. They pass on their observations to **meteorologists**. Spotters can help make tornado warnings more accurate. For example, **radar** might show circular motion, or rotation, in a storm, but that's not always correct. A spotter can confirm this.

✓ risk of injury

✓ unpredictable

✓ hard to find

A tornado is a violently swirling column of air. The strongest tornadoes can have winds of more than 483 kilometres (300 miles) per hour. They are able to pick up cars and throw them like toys! But they can be hard to find. Even experienced chasers might only see a tornado in one out of every five or ten chases.

- ✓ extreme wind and flooding
- ✓ predictable
- ✓ easy to find

Hurricanes are huge storms that form over the ocean. They produce strong winds that rotate around the centre, or eye, of the storm. Hurricane winds can reach speeds of more than 241 km (150 miles) per hour. They also bring lots of rain and cause flooding. Because hurricanes are more predictable than tornadoes, they are easier for chasers to find.

- ✔ spend many hours driving
- ✔ difficult driving conditions
- ✔ responsible for keeping people safe

Storm chasing requires a lot of driving! Storm chasers spend many hours in the car seeking out severe weather. You may have to drive through downpours, strong wind and hail. As the driver, it's extremely important to keep your eyes on the road. Accidents have happened due to drivers watching the sky instead of the road.

That? > be the passenger

- ✓ manage a lot of equipment
- ✓ give directions
- ✓ watch sky for sudden weather changes

Many storm chasers travel with radios, phones and computers. The passenger will use these to get updates on the weather. Passengers are also in charge of reading maps and giving the driver directions. It's important to watch the sky. Storms can change suddenly. The passenger may need to guide the driver out of danger.

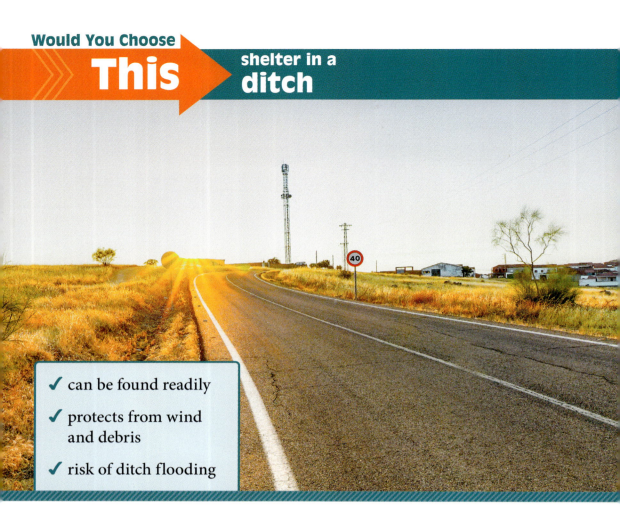

✔ can be found readily

✔ protects from wind and debris

✔ risk of ditch flooding

If you are on the road, trying to drive away from a tornado can be dangerous. Look for a low ditch nearby. Get out of your car and lie down in the ditch. It can protect you from wind and flying **debris**. But be careful if the storm dumps heavy rain. The ditch could flood quickly.

- ✔ protects from wind and debris
- ✔ safer than a vehicle
- ✔ risk of roof falling in

If there's a building nearby, a bathroom can be a safe place during severe weather. If there is a bath, crawl into it. Baths are strong and help keep you protected from flying debris. But if you are travelling with a partner, it might be a tight fight for two. Make sure you cover your head in case the roof comes down.

- ✓ hail can be small or large
- ✓ can damage your car
- ✓ risk of injury

Hail are chunks of ice that develop in a thunderstorm. Depending on their size, they gain speed as they fall from the sky. Most hailstones are tiny – about the size of peas. Some storms can create hailstones the size of tennis balls! These can easily shatter car windscreens. Don't get caught out in the open. Take shelter to stay safe and avoid injury.

✔ one lightning bolt is hotter than the Sun

✔ can strike at a distance

✔ risk of injury or death

Lightning storms can be quite a show. They are also very dangerous. One bolt of lightning can heat the air around it to about 27,760 degrees Celsius (50,000 degrees Fahrenheit). That's about five times hotter than the Sun! Lightning can also strike up to 16 km (10 miles) away from a thunderstorm. Lightning travels extremely fast. You can't dodge a bolt!

This → chase storms in an SUV

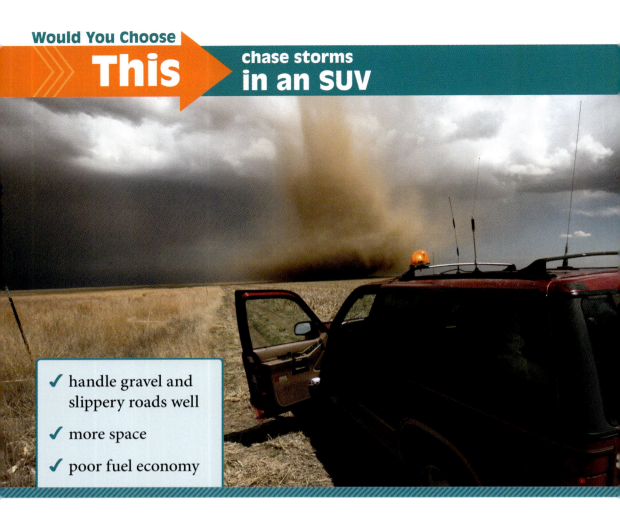

- ✔ handle gravel and slippery roads well
- ✔ more space
- ✔ poor fuel economy

SUVs with four-wheel drive are a popular choice for storm chasers. They can handle gravel roads and slippery conditions. They also have lots of room inside. That's helpful if you are travelling with a team of people and equipment. But SUVs use more fuel than smaller vehicles. You could lose precious time stopping to refuel.

- ✔ good fuel economy
- ✔ cramped space
- ✔ less safe

Some chasers drive for hours when searching for severe weather. Compact cars can save time and money. Better fuel economy means fewer stops to fill up. But they can get cramped if you're travelling with lots of equipment. They are harder to control in bad weather. Plus, some small cars may be less safe than SUVs if there's a crash.

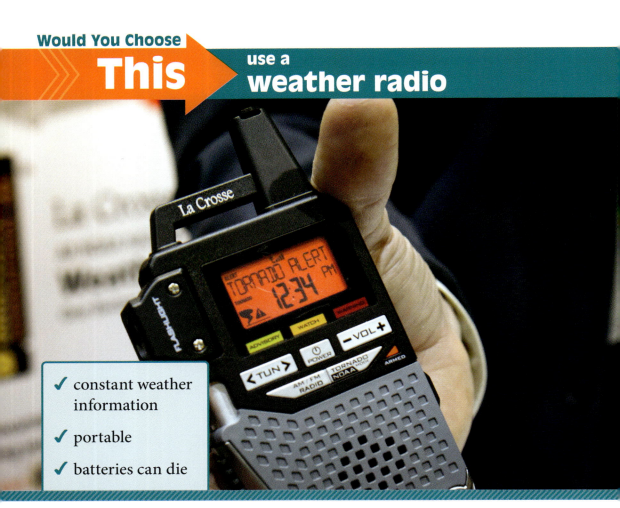

✔ constant weather information

✔ portable

✔ batteries can die

A weather radio broadcasts weather information all day, every day. It reports current weather information and forecasts. It will also alert you if there is a severe weather risk in your area. Weather radios are portable, so you can take them on the road with you. Just make sure you pack extra batteries!

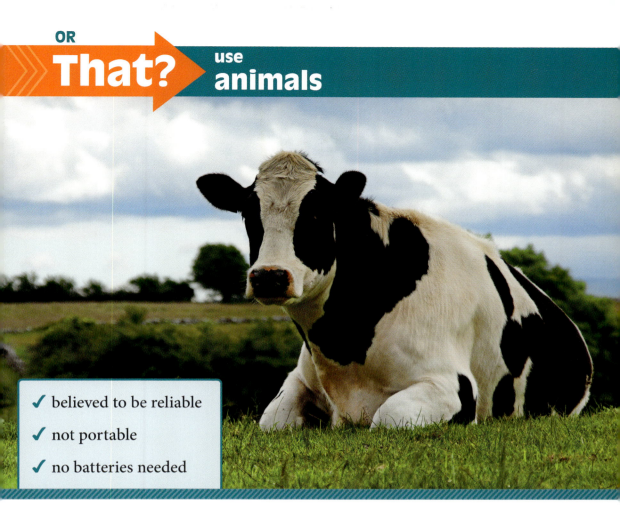

✔ believed to be reliable
✔ not portable
✔ no batteries needed

Animals have been used for hundreds of years to predict weather. Some people believe animals can feel changes in **air pressure**. This means the weather is going to shift. Herd animals stampede towards shelter if a storm is coming. Some scientists believe that cows lie down before it rains.

This ➤ chase storms to **make money**

- ✔ earn money selling photographs or videos
- ✔ exciting but dangerous
- ✔ need expensive equipment

Some people chase storms as part of their career. They take photos and videos of severe weather. They sell them to news organizations and other groups. It's an exciting way to earn money. Not many people get to witness a tornado in action! But this job isn't without risks. And to get high-quality footage, you'll need to spend money on good equipment.

✓ can be dangerous

✓ need special
equipment

✓ help to save lives

There is still a lot about storms that we don't understand. Many deaths happen because there isn't enough warning before a storm hits. Some storm chasers have special equipment that collects data. The closer they can get to the storm, the more information they can collect. Scientists use the information to create more accurate warnings.

This > chase storms in the Great Plains

✓ lots of severe storms

✓ likely to see a tornado

✓ tornadoes can be very strong and dangerous

The Great Plains in the United States are also known as "Tornado Alley". Cold air and warm air collide in this area. This creates strong thunderstorms that can produce tornadoes. On average, about 500 tornadoes hit the Great Plains each year. Some of the strongest and deadliest tornadoes happen in this area.

That? chase storms in Florida

- ✓ good place to find hurricanes
- ✓ tornadoes are weaker
- ✓ likely to see waterspouts

Florida in the United States experiences many types of storms. It has been hit by more hurricanes than any other state in the United States. It is also known for its summer lightning storms. Storm chasers can find weak tornadoes and **waterspouts**. More waterspouts are seen in the Florida Keys than anywhere else in the world.

✔ flooding

✔ risk of illness

✔ risk of injury

A storm surge is ocean water pushed towards the shore by hurricane winds. The water can rise quickly, causing flooding. It can be the deadliest part of a hurricane. The water can be dirty and cause illnesses. Storm surges can also be full of debris, creating a risk of injury. Snakes or alligators have even been brought in with the surge of water.

That?

get caught in a
flash flood

✔ happens quickly

✔ can become trapped

✔ risk of death

Heavy rainfall during a thunderstorm can cause flash floods. This happens when rain falls faster than the ground can absorb it. Flash floods happen within six hours of the rainfall. But they often happen even faster. Flood waters are powerful and dangerous. People can become trapped in their homes or cars. Many deaths occur when people try to drive on flooded roads.

This
partner with an
uninterested driver

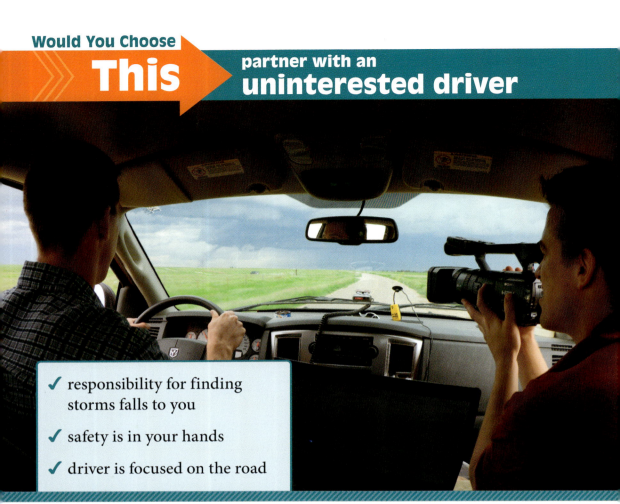

- ✓ responsibility for finding storms falls to you
- ✓ safety is in your hands
- ✓ driver is focused on the road

Storm chasing alone is never recommended. You may have to take a friend who's not interested in weather. A lot will fall on your shoulders. You will have to rely on your own knowledge to find the storms. You will also be responsible for keeping you both out of harm's way. But your friend could make a great driver. He or she is more likely to stay focused on the road instead of watching the sky.

- ✔ led by an expert
- ✔ people in your group may be strangers
- ✔ may not see a storm

Some storm chasing experts offer tours. These are great for people who want to do it but don't have the equipment or knowledge to go alone. Often groups are made up of strangers. The tours can be as long as two weeks and may require hundreds of kilometres of travel. Tour leaders try hard to find a storm. But the weather doesn't always cooperate, and you may not see one at all.

✔ good time to get lightning photos

✔ risk getting lost

✔ could get stuck on flooded roads

Many storms and tornadoes happen at night. Some storm chasers will continue to chase after dark. It's a perfect time to get shots of lightning. The lightning also helps identify the position of the storm. But it can be risky. If you are in an unfamiliar area, you could get lost. It's also harder to see flooded roads.

- ✔ less risk of injury
- ✔ miss out on night-time storms
- ✔ stay rested and ready for more chasing

The danger with storm chasing at night is what you can't see. Downed power cables could be lying across the road. Debris could be flying towards your car. Many chasers call it a day when the sun sets. You might miss out on night-time developments. But you'll get a good night's sleep and be ready to chase storms another day.

Lightning round

Would you choose to . . .

→ pack a lunch **or** stop for food?

→ take photos **or** videos of storms?

→ take a paper map **or** a GPS?

→ get paid **or** chase storms for free?

→ have a mobile phone **or** a satellite radio?

→ stay in a hotel **or** drive hours back home?

→ go to the toilet outside **or** wait to find a public toilet?

Glossary

air pressure force exerted by the weight of the molecules that make up air; usually, the lower the air pressure, the stronger the storm

data information or facts

debris scattered pieces of something that has been broken or destroyed

hail small balls of ice that form in thunderstorm clouds; hail falls from the sky, but the balls of ice are called hailstones when they hit the ground

meteorologist person who studies and predicts weather

monitor keep track of a place or situation

observation gathering of information by watching carefully and taking notice of facts

predict say what you think will happen in the future based on information you have now

radar weather tool that sends out radio waves to determine the size, strength and movement of storms

waterspout mass of spinning cloud-filled wind that stretches from a cloud to a body of water

Find out more

Books

How Do We Predict Weather? (Discover Meteorology), Nancy Dickmann (Raintree, 2021)

It's Raining Fish!: Cool Facts About the Weather (Mind-Blowing Science Facts), Kaitlyn Duling (Raintree, 2019)

Weather (DK Eyewitness), DK (DK Children, 2016)

Websites

www.bbc.co.uk/newsround/21055947
Watch this interview with a storm chaser.

www.dkfindout.com/uk/earth/weather
Find out more about weather.